UPON REFLECTION

Edited by

Sarah Marshall

First published in Great Britain in 2004 by
POETRY NOW
Remus House,
Coltsfoot Drive,
Peterborough, PE2 9JX
Telephone (01733) 898101
Fax (01733) 313524

SB ISBN 1 84460 812 3

FOREWORD

Although we are a nation of poets we are accused of not reading poetry, or buying poetry books. After many years of listening to the incessant gripes of poetry publishers, I can only assume that the books they publish, in general, are books that most people do not want to read.

Poetry should not be obscure, introverted, and as cryptic as a crossword puzzle: it is the poet's duty to reach out and embrace the world.

The world owes the poet nothing and we should not be expected to dig and delve into a rambling discourse searching for some inner meaning.

The reason we write poetry (and almost all of us do) is because we want to communicate: an ideal; an idea; or a specific feeling. Poetry is as essential in communication, as a letter; a radio; a telephone, and the main criterion for selecting the poems in this anthology is very simple: they communicate.

CONTENTS

ABOUT ANYTHING

As times lapse
and oceans arise
and déjà vu
a common surprise
and no one listens
as everyone shouts
faith is found
when all is in doubt
square-shaped gravity
while we sleep in our beds
now learning more
with the nonsense in our heads!

C J Soan

OUR QUEEN OF HEARTS AND CLUBS

Elizabeth, our long-reigned queen,
       like unto 'Good Queen Bess',
Instils in us strong loyalty,
       so her name we gladly bless,
Though Queen of Hearts for knighthoods,
       who her subjects lightly dubs;
Whilst hunting fowl at Sandringham,
       she becomes the Queen of Clubs.

One, two, three, four blows,
       strikes hard the royal stick;
From her gillies and gamekeepers,
       she'd learnt this special trick,
'It's a mercy for the bird,' she says,
       though it isn't very pleasant;
When struck upon the head so hard,
       it's the end of the poor pheasant.

Her Majesty, whose knee is weak,
       now needs her walking stick;
She relies upon it greatly,
       as her leg is not so quick,
If health and strength then weakens,
       and age shows upon her face;
Who will wield the club for her
       to deliver the coup de grace?

Better by far not to be seen,
       to strike the deathly blows;
Remaining to all the noble queen,
       who everybody knows,

Who ages well with dignity,
       and dents not royal charm;
And to royal fowl and animals,
       renders them not any harm.

Edward James Williams
A Bystander Poet

EXPRESSIONS

And were a heart a seed to offer thee,
What flower then, empowers then assume
Such grace, her magic, all her majesty,
Deserves to one so beautiful in bloom;
Sweet flower wandering amid, will soon
These men who cower, hide not in their tongue,
By love's perfume, frequent in heaven's tune,
And blush the air in ointment scent among;
O' rose, a fragrance to impale a heart,
Whose petal, love's impression urge to kiss,
Where men who rhyme sweet flower, love their art,
And words to shy away in lovers' lips;
Are longer still than summer's voice around,
In greater hearts, temptation's love is found.

Christopher W Wolfe

DESTINY

When first we met I had a sense
Of meaningful coincidence.
Our guardian angels had combined
To make quite sure our lives entwined.
If not, then how can we explain
A meeting which would set in train
Such closeness, just as if we knew
A previous bond would continue
With shared adventure, laughter, fun,
A web of love and trust fine spun
To keep us linked in harmony,
Companions by destiny.

Evelyn Westwood

IF ONLY, IF

If only, if, the world was paradise,
A heaven with a sky so bright and blue,
If only, if, we saw through angels' eyes.

Each day the news is bad and someone dies,
A plaque, a war, the innocents we slew,
If only, if, the world was paradise.

We all make mistakes, after we are wise,
Through life we walk, decisions sometimes rue, ·
If only, if, we saw through angels' eyes.

Each day's routine of work, no play, sunrise,
A yoke we wear, happiness overdue,
If only, if, the world was paradise.

Some nation's rich, some poor, what sacrifice,
Will humanity share its wealth with you?
If only, if, we saw through angels' eyes.

The rich aloof to equality's prize,
To share the world's new wealth a simple view,
If only, if the world was paradise,
If only, if we saw through angels' eyes.

David M Walford

SURVIVORS

When I think of Paestum and the cloudless days
We wandered there, it is the lizards'
Dazzling bodies which come at once to mind.
Far from camouflaging their existence
Chameleon-like in grey-green fustiness,
They seemed determined that the sun should turn
Their darting movements into flashing blue,
Turquoise and emerald streaks of brilliance.
The reptilian bravado inspired
Perhaps by occupation of the site
In timeless residence, aeons before
The temples of the ancient gods were built.
Glorious once in pristine magnificence
Before Christ's birth, only a pediment
And stately Doric columns now remain,
Their gigantic measurements reducing
Clambering tourists to minute proportions.
Ruined remnants - they are yet majestic
And resonate unyielding pagan pride
In their survival, their antiquity.
The worshippers of Graeco-Roman gods
Have long since perished. So too these structures
In time will crumble or events destroy;
But down among the scattered broken stones,
Or on some recumbent, sun-warmed pillar
In triumph basking, will still be lizards.

Sheila Watts

FOR ONLY THEN . . .

My heart is pleading for one more caress.
It beats against me in angry need
In hope to feel your hands upon my chest
For only then,
My heart will rest.

My eyes are pleading for one more glance,
They pour a river in insistent need
Just one more glance that I can keep
For only then,
My eyes will sleep.

My lips are pleading for one more kiss,
They lie here dead in lonely need.
The kiss of life to last a while
For only then,
My lips will smile.

My body hurts,
It needs you here,
It needs to feel your body near
For it is only then . . . I will feel complete
Two bodies at one
Two bodies to keep

Jodi Wheeler

PEACOCKS

Three peacocks strutted across my friend's lawn!
Will her next visit be from a deer and its fawn?
(Santa and his reindeer - Rudolph).

Christine M Wicks

ODE TO INSOMNIA

It's 4am in the morning,
And I'm wide wake again,
With another attack of insomnia,
And eyes that are bloodshot with pain.
I'm fed up with tossing and turning,
My bed is in a right mess,
The amount of sleep I get these days,
Seems to be less and less.
My eyes are casting shadows,
Where there were none before,
I think I might try and meditate,
Maybe that's the cure.
If not I'll try the chemist,
And get some sleeping pills,
They're bound to have a cure,
That'll solve my sleeping ills.
I'm going back to bed now,
To try and get some sleep,
I think I'll try that age-old trick,
Where you relax and count sheep.

Donna Salisbury

ON STEPPING OVER A DRUNK

You can't notice me as I step around you,
Your blonde hair laced dirtily across your face.
I wonder are you even conscious but
You slide and writhe so you must be.
How many men will try and rip
Through the papered flesh of your tights?
Move your legs however they choose?
You have no control.
Your clothes are dirty, stinking,
Reeking of mud, fags and alcohol.
I can't even see your face,
You could be quite pretty,
I don't know.
I'd like to help you but how can I?
Pull you to your feet for you to slide
Back down again?
Put you in a taxi?
Do you even know where you live?
Your name? Yourself?
Your clothes, once chosen and bought,
Barely cover your senseless body,
Your red heels glitter pathetically
On your feet.
There's nothing I can do for you
But step over.

Jillian Shields

ENGLAND

It has no new bones to bear
Only fieldwork that has been dug before,
A pretence encased in chicken-wire -
The cortisone of piled history books that are drained blue
Removing a red thick cotyledon from a tired seed -

It is a tired man's overcoat heavy with rain
That greets a long needed summer and blooming flower beds.

It is deeper than the underpinning
Cracking of a concrete slab -
Bites as a cancerous spine,
Congealed foods thrown to the masses as spin
Blinding us beggars losing heart on a decaying pearl.

It is a cracked knuckle, thick skinned from
Years of digging over with blunted tools.

It should let the rain fall without guilt
Tie ropes to the sun so that it cannot set
And photograph every screaming inch
For the sake of posterity,
Before the seas come

Remembered the right way.

Stuart Springthorpe

GRAINS OF SAND

In bustling farewell
They leave their vast shimmering family root.
A white-gold heartless mother
Who spills her endless blood carelessly
Never yearning for her children's return.
Characterless babes save their subtle shading,
Tossed in the wind as seeds from a farmer's bib.
Each one to new ground
But for what purpose these?
Save that of whipping the face or blinding the eye.
Hand in hand with banshee wind
Flailing, hurling, rising and thrashing
They sing and screech like flocks of frenzied starlings at dusk
Then plummet earthward only to rise again and again
Revellers in an endless frenzied joy.

Anna Shannon

PARASOL

Beneath the parasol
lies another day, spent
in anxious concern:
what to eat, to drink,
to wear.
How to arrange important
affairs - how to pay
credit cards.
Cut up the cards.
Too late, too late.
So continues the cycle
beneath the parasol
of life.

Dawn Sansum

OUR ENGLAND AND HEROES OF FRANCE 1998

Off to France they went, in the summer of ninety-eight,
On their backs rode a nation's hope.
The royal family was rooting for them,
The upper classes were rooting for them,
Us plebs were rooting for them,
Indeed the whole nation was rooting for them.

They had their Hermes and Paris,
Fleet of foot, stylish, tenacious,
They had their Achilles too, with a heel to match.
And Achilles raised his heel once too often
And a Danish pastry did for him.

We all know what Danish pastries are like,
Tasty, scrumptious, yum, yum,
But, oh so deadly for the midriff,
And deadly was that Danish pastry
For the England midfield.
Up went Achilles' heel, down tumbling came a nation's hope
And our brave lads were on their way home.

Don't be too hard on him, Achilles, I mean,
He's only a lad, his, a painful lesson well-learnt.

Home they came, not as villains, mind
But heroes all, all of them,
Achilles, Hermes, Paris, among them
To live and fight another day.
Four years is not long
Their very best they will give, we know,
And maybe this time, maybe
The World Cup, the precious gold cup,
Will come home to England,
The natural and spiritual home of football, we hope.

Scholastica Bennin-Sam

BUTTERFLY

Wafer wing silken tremor
filled with pedantic flutter
a butterfly spun a thousand threads of gossamer
across a Spanish plain
flying across a sea of faces
in sun, sea, sand.

It will one day land on a French bougainvillaea
with a tremor of its wafer-wing
warming its petals 'neath
a Mediterranean sun
will its fragile frame be crudely crushed forever
the elusive butterfly pursues eternity . . .

kissing the dying
embracing the untouched
with its tenderness.

It will unwind a tortured heart
and calm the waves of endless whys.
Is this not the fountain spray
soaring through time
to splash eternity in my eyes
and a door flung wide
to open it?

Judy Studd

PREHISTORIC PYGMY FOOTPRINT

into the span of her palm
the abstruse pebble easily slid;
it was the size of a diminutive foot
and must have travelled
to this sparse spot with the surge and
the flow of the river Esk

its curves, smooth as bum-fluff,
possessed no corns nor snags;
the sole of it was bare of any
blemish - it was a petrified print
of a prehistoric past - indeed
its dimensions, humbled us.

A E S Gamage

SOMEONE UNKNOWN

Someone unknown turns,
Someone between us at sleep.

An impulse, inflict
Or . . .
Rebel, revenge!

Someone unknown sighs,
Moan at dine.

A murmur, a misery,
Maybe a . . .
Malice, mischief!

Someone unknown steps,
In wardrobe,
Dressing table, trunk.
Arrogance, shame,
Perhaps a . . .
Disgrace, danger!

Shuvra Rahman

THE BEAUTY OF SYMMETRY

Maybe there is a biological explanation
maybe it is just an aesthetic rule
that God or whosoever has created
the animal kingdom decided that
we should all be that way
I cannot believe it is the result
of a sheer accident.
Why do we have two eyes
separated by a nose
two arms and two legs
in perfect symmetry
when our innards are set
at random, or so it appears?
It's as if that deity of nature
or however you may wish to call it
wanted to hide
the functions of life
the way we do when
we build a car
concealing its motor
under a hood
and making sure
the outer body
is as pleasing to the eye
as we can render it.
Look at the ugliest of reptilians
and you will find that common trait.
What would we have looked like
if we just had a transparent
envelope covering our entrails?
Would we still be beautiful?

Albert Russo

POSTERITY

September 1st . . . already.
Sunday.
Sunny! Quiet.
Clock ticks on.
Mind feels awake with how things are,
quiet, before the day's plans become reality.
Bedroom,
forever in a state of being dealt with;
the job gets interrupted by other tasks
in a busy life . . . until I need to sleep.

Even my notebook here,
empty, or so I thought,
contains a couple of pages of another's handwriting,
the meanderings of a stressed loved one,
now, no longer here, lost, gone.
She tried to 'sort things out in her head' too.
And now, I'm doing the same.

This new notebook, fat,
inviting blank pages,
is really twenty years old.
One day, like the writer,
it will be destined for . . .
                    somewhere else;
                    the soil, burning,
                    returning to dust particles.
My thoughts, anxieties will, then, be for nothing.
Memories of me will be in others.
And my written works, as poems, stories,
observations or fiction, may last a bit longer.

Unless some foolish leader gets up one morning,
fails to have *his* moment at *his* notebook,
            writing out *his* anxieties,

fails to have *his* cornflakes and whose hands still tremble
        from last night's alcoholic binge and,
accidentally,
leans against *his* ego's red button,

and we are no more,
with
no
more
hope . . .

Jerome Kiel

GEORGE

For
all the complaining
old George did -

'The cold,
the damp,
the wet,
the snow,'

He lays now
deep
in the thick of it -
where
no man
would want to go.

No
breath of air
shall
chill him now,
no
'noise' of earth
shall
pierce his ears,
sadly,
when
George was live,
he had been dead
for years.

Diana Mudd

LIES

Silence
Broken by the final gasps
Of feelings hit
With absolute impunity
By you

Deafening
The magnitude
Of every word you fit
Into the shameful lies
That you still spew.

Kim Montia

THE HOLIDAY IN

The best wee place in Scotland has not just scenery,
It's a little piece of heaven, it's called Mary's B & B.
And when we're feeling weary and need a little rest,
We head off up to Mary's where the company's the best.
You'll always find a welcome of warmth to meet you there.
No matter what the weather, there's no chill in Mary's air.
When we first met we had no way of knowing what we'd find,
But it didn't take too long to see that she was sweet and kind.
Her standards she keeps very high, your priorities come first,
So if you want to make a friend, meet oor Mary at Penhurst.

Elizabeth McNeil

THIS BED

Darkness falls
Between these four walls,
A curse laid upon this bed,
As she bawls,
The infection crawls,
Up and through her head.

Sanity lost,
Together lovers pay the cost,
A curse laid upon this bed,
She was crossed,
Now eyes cold as frost,
Gaze across the 'stead.

Antony Milne

ON FREEDOM'S WINGS

She glides and soars . . .
This America of ours . . .
Through skies of black and blue . . .
Over hills and prairies too . . .
On freedom's wings . . .
America sings . . .

Leaving her nest
This country so blest,
At times dipping low . . .
Wondering which way to go . . .
On freedom's wings . . .
America sings . . .

Eagles' wings begin to stir . . .
With God closely watching over her . . .
No difficulties insurmountable . . .
She rises high . . .
Flying in the sky . . .
On Freedom's wings . . .
America sings . . .

Carol Olson

SCHIZOPHRENIA

Buy two
Receive a pair
Free
Or vice versa.

Michael Phillips

CARNAL LUST

I know someone said that sex is overrated,
But it's nights without it I've always hated.

Hated to be without some carnal pleasure,
Nights of pure lust I'll always treasure.

Treasure moments with one and moments with many,
At this moment right now, I'd settle for any.

Sharon Grimer

WILLOW

Willow I love you
Willow I care
Baby I will always
Be there
For you.
Mother Nature took
You away,
Now you're not alive
I know my baby
That you were
Only five.
I still have your sister
Freia.
Hopefully she'll live long.
I'm always thinking of you
Even though
You're gone.

Maxene Huntley

CROSSROAD

An honorific speech
The worthy were assembled.
Protestors in the balconies
Flashpoint
Men were angered.

The militant nightmare
Keeps coming true.
The myth of security
Hanging
By threads so few.

Must we embrace chaos
Or live and work as one?
Dissociate from the warmongers
Crossroads
For all our sons.

John Hobbs

WATERED TOMATOES

He used to treat them like children;
his Wenallt tomatoes.
He'd strain sheep manure,
lovingly gathered
from the damp mountainside
in old hessian sacks,
in a tin bath
flush with rainwater.

And the tomatoes,
the sweetest I'd ever tasted;
would sip the brown liquid
from the soft soil
like sugared tea.

Marc Harris

HE DIDN'T COME HOME TO DINNER

Lois settled down to her coffee and bagel,
This her quiet time when, hair in rollers,
She caught up on yesterday's news,
Read her bits of mail and
Drained the last dregs of Maxwell House.
She winced at the press photos of little girls
Being terrorised on their walk to school.
Distant relatives in the old country
Could never enjoy the freedom she had.
Humming, she reiterated Sinatra's sentiments,
'New York, New York, it's a wonderful town!'

She heard Wilbur running the shower about six.
A good boy, he tried so hard not to wake her,
But she was so familiar with his routine since joining
The World Trade Centre on Lower Manhattan.
He'd laugh at how quickly he soared
To his office on the ninety-fifth floor
After fender to fender traffic across the Brooklyn Bridge.
A proud mom, the same thought crossed her mind regularly,
'Wish he'd find a nice girl - still plenty of time!'

She'd prepare him a nice dinner for six-thirty.
His favourite - meat loaf, mashed sweet potato
And her speciality, creamy Florida coleslaw.
The clock chimed nine - so stuffy in this kitchen.
She stepped out on the fire-escape,
Never tiring of the view, those magnificent twin towers!
'Oh God, what thick black smoke billowing from one,
And why is that aircraft veering so low?'
Her heart lurched as, across the East River, her son's stopped!

8.30pm - the meat loaf was still unsliced!

Pat Heppel

IN THE PHILHARMONIC

A famous pub this,
Mainly for its latrines,
Made of porcelain, they say,
Witnessed many scenes.

It's a continuing 'Play For Today',
Pool of life - lads and lasses,
A gathering of the chattering classes.

Next door they discuss the price of clothes,
(M & S of course)
The ladies excitedly chatter,
Safe values of 'Middle England',
In a bastion of Left Wing belief.

Is this what pubs used to be like
Before the disco revolution?
When Tebbit's dad got on his bike,
Or was it just an illusion?

Time for thought and conversation,
Not for me though, I'm alone,
Thinking of the state of the nation,
Of paper, wood and stone.

The ladies tinkle the gin and tonic
And discuss in earnest
Young Liz and Jamie's career prospects,
Such are the dilemmas
Between the same and opposite sex.

All one in the Philharmonic.

P Higgins

THE MAN BEHIND THE DOOR

The elderly are all at risk
Who sit at home alone,
Some of them, they have no locks,
Some of them, they have no phone.

Beware the man behind the door
For he is there awaiting,
To get inside and rob you of
The things that took a lifetime creating.

They come in with an excuse like,
'Can I come in and read your meter?'
Or, 'Hello, I'm doing a survey
And my name is Honest Peter.'

So don't be taken in by
All their banter and politeness,
Or you may find your life and home
Loses all its brightness.

So remember this next time you hear
Them on your door a-knocking,
If you don't know that friendly voice,
Then keep your chair a-rocking.

M Havard

MOTHER'S ANGUISH

My son, oh my son -
I hear your plea with heavy heart
It renders my heart apart
I want you so; your father too.

There is no conspiracy,
No malice; no ugly intent
I have to do what I must
Not for me, not for your father; just for you
As my sinking heart knows the fact
And your father too.

I know you have aspirations beyond imagination
I know your desire to reach infinite heights
That will make a mother proud.

But my son, my darling son -
We know something that you don't -
It's not your fault, nor is it ours
Doctor says it's God's will
That your existence must end -
As your aspirations will not aspire
Heights that you dream of will not be reached.

So my son,
I hope you understand your mother's anguish
I hope you forgive the use of my right
To put an end to your existence for reasons clear.
Goodbye, my son.

A Jamil

LIGHT AND LIGHT AGAIN

Light and light again;
all in the lost darkened eyes I cannot see;
blinded now by the cloak
upon my face;
upon that other, binary,
sight of reality.
It is the thrust of black flowers
in the void -
not the absence of light
when the hollow moon soars.
The glow of the night-sun
warms us yet.

And we in the shade
of the velvet,
pay our tolls
in some small diligence:
cradled in shadows of shadows;
touching
the light, and light again,
here at the feet of morning.

Peter Jones

REMEMBER ME

Remember me
      I was the one that would play the games
when no one else would come around. I was the dead
cowboy on the floor, Lone Ranger's partner or the
customer at the door.

Remember me,
      I was the one that made castles with your
pillows and wrapped those warm sturdy walls around you
at night so you would drift into your land of make-believe
with your protective armour shining bright.

Remember me
      I am the one that wiped away those tears, I
sat you upon my knee and wrapped my arms around you
tight until you felt safe enough to smile and throw away
the fears.

Remember me
      I was the one that was there when you tripped
and hurt your knee. I would put a magic plaster on and the hurt
would be gone, the scratch you could no longer see.

Remember me
      I am the one that held all your insecurities in the
palm of my hand and sorted them out, one by one, until
they were all gone.

Remember me
      Well I am still here, inside I am still the same,
although you can't see. Now I cry the tears. I feel the pain
and carry all the insecurities. How times have changed, please!
Remember me.

Dianne Audrey Daniels

THE THRUST AND PARRY OF LOVE

Two by two, into the ark of the unknown
we willingly subject ourselves,
throwing ourselves into the belly of the surf,
breathing, against the leviathan's kiss,
we turn and tumble, laugh and cry.

This is how it starts: the lust of the thrust;
hot and humid, heavy with expectation,
curling the toes, grating the teeth,
a beautiful dark angel hugging the magical margins
of the only-half-hoped-for.

Then the parry: a lie, lip-deep and bitter,
staining the air with its indelible infidelity;
the frosty halo of winter choking everything
that was Eve-expectant and Eden-beautiful.
Each way now as steep as a grave.

Two by two, into the ark of the unknown
we willingly subjected ourselves,
to reach this - the foaming final furlong.
How do we decide? When each step into the dark
lessens the light that could lead us to our beds?

Even the almanac stars cannot predict how it will end.

Andrew Detheridge

EZE VILLAGE

High in the hills of Provence,
Nestled on a craggy tor,
Sleeps the ancient village of Eze.
It clings as an eagle's claw.
Living and dead share the eyrie,
Eking living a daily care.
Headstones bear silent witness
To all who've lived and died there.

The streets are narrow and stony.
The houses almost kiss overhead.
On the apex, a garden of cactus
And a breeze to clear the head.
For one brief moment I came
And breathed in the still summer air.
I reflected, like many before me,
On the hardy who first settled there.

Patricia Adele Draper

WHERE ONIONS TAKE YOU

The brass-cleaning solution
Was like condensed milk
With an odd smell.

Thick ivory liquid,
Tipped meticulously from its posh can
Tinted clean pink cloths,
Greyed by the rubber's fingers.

Little Dutch girl with buckets
Was first,
The dullness of her skirts
Polished with sharp words
Into golden furls.

In the scullery
Clumps of onions were draped
Hot in their mustering stink.
Teased out from the allotment that day
Like newborns
Mothered in mud
Soft, bronzing.

On whistles,
Whippets sped down the ship canal,
Pell-mell elastic dog-distortions
Contorting tight past sheet-iron bulking
Dislodging, at kill-fury speed,
Rust fragments from the old steamer.

Ocean salts corrode
Metal membranes
Revealing, like old pickled onions
In a pickle jar
Bruises, blemishes and discolouration

But that is in the layers,
In the skins,

How are we when the lemon sunsets
Fall to pieces?

Phil Fox

JUST ONE MISTAKE

Should 'just one mistake' be the end of time
True love in this line send but must try rhyme
When all watch universe guided by the wise
Just become a broken away fraction realise
But never have two wrongs made one right
Take the sun away will be everlasting night
Collect by law from poor help the very rich
Will only cause another hole like tank ditch
Our country is sponsoring corruption no tale
Rather than a fair hearing give them more bail
This fair to veterans who served country well
Should end a life in bitter scrawl, and cold hell.

Many this Christmas will be very cold and bleak
Many aged with despair will their master meet
A mistaken bid for freedom and independence
Rest of life will join our service of remembrance
To make more pay, please remember forever
Your biggest mistake, with love find not clever
Do rockets and blasting comply, ever make sense
Threatening more walls with barbed wire high fence
Ignorance cause deaths which world has tasted
How many lives are given honoured but wasted
Ask you to change rectify universe biggest mistake
Before millions more hearts fill with bitter hate break.

John Flint

EXCALIBUR

I lie in the rushes and sedges
On the edge of Dozemary Pool,
They rustle and whisper,
And move in the breeze,
Like a skeleton army band.

The sun glows soft
Through the veils of mist
As golden day appears.

A gold light touches the ripples
On the surface of Dozemary Pool.
Ripples! Now I know.

Slowly a silver handle,
Studded with rarest jewels,
A silver blade drips diamonds,
A slender hand holds it aloft.

Excalibur lives! And now I know
That Arthur will soon return.

Sheila Giles

AN EMPTY PURSE

To face tomorrow must be very hard
For the majority who luxuries are barred.
Those whose men have been out of work for years,
Whose every evening is the same, ending it in tears.
Children dressed in charity clothes,
Their classmates sticking up their nose,
Shoes so old and worn that you can see
The children's sockless toes.
No treats or designer clothes you will find
In this ramshackle house,
There is so little food that you will never see a single mouse.
Depression has set in, the outlook gets worse,
There is no hope with three kids and an empty purse.

Don Goodwin

SEPTEMBER BLUES

S   eptember two - the day of my birth
E   motions tug at my childhood past
P   onder over young jelly parties
T   houghts change, disappear like a musical chair
E   nergy now ring o' roses collapsed
M   emories sit in coloured hundreds and thousands
B   lack moods, fester into red dreams
E   lements of the before, sliced like a lit, candled cake
R   ecall the screaming gaiety of the long gone party throng

B   ut now many years later
L   ying in window wait for that Royal Mail
U   nsure of who will recall this day
E   xactly like last year he rode straight through
S   eems I am forgotten, no postage due.

Ian Bowen

FOR WES

They carry out experiments
on rats, then make a fuss,
and claim so many things are bad,
or dangerous for us.
Should we take any notice?
You don't need a degree
to see that rats are different
from the likes of you and me.
We don't grab lunch from litter bins,
nor live in rubbish tips,
and we don't invade the sewers
for aquatic weekend trips!
I'll listen to the experts' words,
but then I may ignore
their findings, and well-meant advice -
they really can't be sure.

While I'm on the subject of the rat,
well, here's a thought.
We read in books about the plagues,
and pestilence he brought.
Now, are we being reasonable,
or is it only me,
who thinks it harsh to blame the rat -
why don't we blame the flea?

Paul F Burch

THINGS STAY THE SAME

You are compulsive
All or nothing

You snap at me
And you are angry

I am unable
To talk to you

You don't listen
To me

Frustrated and lonely
I write it down

And nothing changes
Because you don't read it

And things stay the same!

Moira Jean Clelland

ETHIOPIA - 20 YEARS ON?

I have my pen and paper ready to portray
But one must ask, what right do I have?
To personally publish millions of destitute others' indescribable
misery?
Fortunate enough to go to the gym today, to watch TV, buy a burger
What right do I have? I was ten years old, I remember, maybe
that's why
1984 took one man to wake our world to fortunate others,
like myself
This great one awoke us to what we all dismiss, this world we do share.

Eyes fixated on images of dying souls with dusted rags - hell on earth
Cradling bundles of bones, too lethargic to wipe the flies
The flies that lie in wait for the predictable death
Not even a shovel to bury the loved ones
Bare hands of the dying were burying the dead-horrific

Aid camps playing God, selecting mouths that should be fed,
not by choice
Choice would have meant chance for all
Desperate as it may seem but why feed the soon to be dead?
Feed the strong to get them stronger, aid the sick to get them fitter
Cruelty had to be such a harsh devastation

Sadly, superstition meant 'hide the children from the devil'.
But these children soon were to be dead, a cruel injustice
Blame could easily be awarded for hiding these children
But without the given right of education, they are forgiven

A country shrouded in war and political promise
A country that solely relied on the blessing
The western world with so much grain surplus - it was a mess
Time running out for men, women and children, survival was
simply . . . time

We all remember, we can't forget, but today the plight is even stronger
20 years on and another realistic disaster looms - its drought again
The only hope is, the world reflects as before
That the children of our today, stop and stare just as I did!

Amanda Carley

YOUR MOTHER PHONED

The office ladies, faces all concerned,
Usher me into the reprographics room
Where the copier's mechanical mantra
Might serve as a screen.
There, Barbara said you'd phoned –
The word . . . you know, never used.
We talked instead about how long
It was since your first mastectomy.
I said you'd joked about
Buying a bra in any size you liked
Now. And all the while
The copying machine must have been
Duplicating multiplying sheets of
I know not what. Before
Barbara asked me where I was going
Now. And I assured her
I was all right - *I had a union meeting.*

Kate Symons

FRONT FEELINGS

If I were strong and tough
And vicious too
I'd live with hardcase roughnecks
At the front.
Bayoneting enemy shock troops to death.
You'd see me with my horrible
Maniacal face
Leading the van in every bayonet charge
Hounding the shattered enemy to death
'Worthless scum,' I'd say
'You have no fight left in you at all.
We'll take your homes and land,
And women too!'
And when the war was o'er
And the foe well dead,
I'd live with valiant warriors,
And well fed.

Philip Corbishley

IS THERE STILL A FIRE?

Is there still a fire,
And I the tinder of its flame,
As it used to be;
Is it burning now;
Does it, with fury, rage inside
When you're next to me -

Or, not fire, but ice,
And I the winter of its freeze;
Have your flames now frozen
Into icicles,
Unthawing when I'm next to you,
Where *my* flame still grows?

Harry Crompton-fils

GIRL, AFRICAN

She walks in with a parcel
of stuffed fish-heads and yams
and begins washing up while they warm
and casually sucks one of the eyes
while I open the wine and watch her
take off the trainers that make her limp.

Her smile pretends to like my music
and there's the usual bedroom struggle
to remove her clothes
until she clamps my wrist
and I notice the rag around her waist
which she wears for fasting.
And she still hasn't spoken a word.

I remind her that last month
it was the blood that had stopped her
because it was against her beliefs
and now it's *more* religion, and will it,
I ask, be a headache next time?

She dresses swiftly,
her Nefertiti head upright and still
and with a flat-vowelled finality
suggests I write a poem about it,
and soundlessly leaves the house.

Ken Champion

SAD EYES

Her eyes, so beautiful,
Sapphire blue sprinkled with amber lights,
Where a thousand pictures reflect
Moods and memories
Of years past.

But today the blue eyes are misted
With tears
As she comes to terms
With the grief she is feeling and
Memories
Almost too hard to bear.

Sad eyes,
Deep in thoughtful remembrance,
Reflecting on the past.
Sad eyes,
Afraid of what the future may bring.

Judy Rochester

THE BRIDGE

Towards the colliery tips
        occasional remembered trains
mornings, afternoons; commonplace,
           just passing, a fact there.

Clouds and trains, scurrying past,
          now locked in the past.
Hard Engineering bricks,
patina burnished by time and atmosphere
           accretions of inky soot.

The bridges, immense and earthed
          to this child
by no means extinct
still fairly new
still
sustaining the passage of heavy trains.

They were built in 1899,
         the end of Victorian modernity,
         a modernity, that of my grandfather.

John T Roberts

REALISATION

Silently, she slipped away
slipped into a box
marked 'Memories'.
Were they good?
Or bad?
Will they fade with time
or stay silently inside
a crowded mind?
This memory could last . . .
Lock the box
throw away the key
slip away
silently.

Greta Robinson

DISAPPOINTMENT

Disappointment knocks at my door
clamouring winds
loudly proclaiming
'Let me in,'
and time ticks
against the reality
of you,
never forgetting
a promise made
in the hour
before you embraced
obscurity.

Carla Iacovetti

MOTHER RUSSIA

Like that too with you
Gone out of the city
Flattery pretty missy
All left behind with the group
Trendy Wendy spoke out
Called out *Mother Russia*
Stop the flow of blood into the Volga
Murmurings in the heart also spoken about
Bullying man the 'also ran'
Myself close by the sea an apartment for me
Mother Russia from our sorrows shades of light save us
From peril give us shelter from the storm
To pay in equal parts.

S M Thompson

EDUCATION

This is education
The answer for the nation
Knowledge is the remedy
To alleviate the frustration

The building is the school
What I'm teaching is the rule
The only way out
Become a master with a tool

Because this is the plight
Children fuss and fight
Like fools in the dark
Each one searching for the light

And where is the key
Keep on searching you'll see
Climb to the top, to the university

The highest stage
Don't stop working!
Turn the page
When you grow old
You'll be as knowing as your age

Education is in store
Don't have enough?
Then take some more
Fill your thoughts with learning
You'll be much better than before.

A Brown

NO ONE IS LISTENING TO THE CRIES OF THE CHILD

The child comes home
from their day in hell.
School it is known as.
Physical and mental abuse
is all that the day had in store.
Aren't these supposed to be the
best days of our lives? So we
are told. No one is listening
to the cries of the child.

Lay your head down to sleep,
so many tears to cry, so much
pain to try and ease. The day
is repeated in slow motion, as
my eyes are shut. Morning comes
not much sleep had. Another day
in hell lies ahead. No one is
listening to the cries of the child.

Another day filled with physical
and mental abuse. People see, but
do not speak, just stand and stare
with a smile on their face. These
people call themselves human beings.
No one is listening to the cries of the child.

So many times spoke to adults, only
to be treated like I was in the wrong,
to want the pain and suffering to stop.
Only to be told be a good child and run
along. No one is listening to the cries
of the child.

Can't take this torture anymore, I lay
my head down to sleep, no more pain,
no more tears.

Now you're listening, now you're listening,
but now you're listening too late. Failed
the child that walked through your doors
and into your care. Let that forever be
on your minds. You tell that child's parents.
Why?

Something is wrong with this world.
Now you're listening.

Gillian McKinley

JUST KEEP TRYING

Very good,
You might just amaze me,
If you just keep trying,
Some say I'm too thick-skinned for my own good,
Just look me in the eye,
Intimidating?
To the point that no one gets close,
Not even my own father,
I feel I need this,
To protect a fragile core,
That bruises with the greatest ease,
Knock me down,
If you hit me hard enough,
These walls may crumble,
But I could go with them,
So choose your weapon with care,
I can only take so much,
Do it the right way,
And this love inside will be yours.

Richard Ward

MENTAL ILLNESS

Cross the teeth of the land in war
Up and down, in and out
Of these deep trenches
In the twilight.
In a time of trouble
I have staggered
Dazed and wounded
In a shock walk
To get to a hospital.
I have found level ground
And am surprised
To see grass with the mud
The gunfire still pricks my ears
And addles my brain
In recorded remembrance.
Could it be that this is the end
Of all that iron and violence?
I will not speculate the possibility of it,
Only to walk onwards, forward and away.
The smoke in the air is disappearing and it is cloudy.
The ground, the trees I see in the distance
Are ashen-brown.

Thomas Conor

SHE GALLOPED UPON OCCUPIED BEACHES

Onlookers, tired of observing
The hoof marks made by her
White stallion, entreated her until
She dismounted her steed. (there
Were witnesses who maintained
That beach-goers had threatened her.)

She dismounted her steed and looked
Around at the carnival-like atmosphere that
Had surely swallowed up the fragile seashells
And had driven away the stone crabs. She saw
Concessions with rainbow-coloured umbrellas,
Quarrelling children with neon-zinc noses, and

Bare-breasted women who were topless
Until the next security patrol upon the beach.
She saw hotdogs with five different types of
Mustard, and French fries with as many different
Shapes. She sought the solace of a clump of
Reeds; so she could rest and figure all of this out.

The reed clusters were surrounded by cigarette
Wrappers and gum wrappers, and by the vibrating
Lyrics of gangster rappers, so that she was unable to
Sort out anything. While she was trying to think, a kite
Landed in her hair like a psychedelic bird's nest. With
No need for further thought, she reasoned that she was

Better off on her white stallion, and she galloped into the
Ocean. No one tried to save her. All were wearied by her
White steed, her galloping foray and the hoof marks indicating
That she had been there. As in history, the ebb and flow of life had
Erased all traces of her, with her bothersome reminder of a
Past where waters were clear and nature was to be revered.

Alice Parris

DRIVERS AT DUSK

White headlights, red tail-lights,
Cars moving slowly in line.
A metal snake of jammed-up cars
Sullenly, wearily curse the road ahead.
Yellow saucers suspended lamplight
A blue and white 'get in lane' sign.
Green for go, the pedestrians have gone
Dark shadows lay idle on the road.
Past billboards and seductive words
Down a side street a lamplight strobes.
The sky is now a highlighted mauve
All that remains of the day is leaving.
Two lovers kiss in the hazy heat
Turn the radio on, let the mood swing.
Red buses, window heads, flat faces
Dream of sunsets and exotic places.

Paul Willis

IT TOLLS FOR THEE

The time had arrived. He shivered.
He felt so alone.
He had only picked at his last meal before . . .
The priest heard his confession.
'Forgive me Father, for I have sinned.'
'Why am I not at peace?' he thought.
'After all, I am innocent,
I have done no wrong!'

He is now surrounded by all those
Who must witness the ordeal.
Suddenly, the grim-faced governor
Touches him on the shoulder and
Asks him earnestly,
'Are you ready, Mr Executioner?'

Peter Davies

STRANGE EXPERIENCE OUTSIDE AN INN

Springtime animation manifest in every
Leaf and all kinds of blossomings,
Calls forth a sort of heavenly glamour
In every feature of the evergreen heath
Close to the forest dark and deep!
A constant sense of awakening from
Winter trance and failure I feel
In all features of the dead surroundings;
The evening soon draws on, and I step
Out of my hilly home, descend
Into the wider valley, and stand beside
The pool of a pond, watching and hearing
All the genuine stir of resurrection in nature;
A timid animal world has come to life
For the season in bloom quite pristine!
Little tadpoles begin to bubble up through
The water silent, with toads' noises
Coming up like very young ducks;
Winter has still dragged out,
The last dregs of winter seem persisting still!
Immediately I scale down the higher vale,
And enter an inn for comfort and relief
By blazing hearth, keeping out the cold outside;
Dancing at bar with a musical concert inside
Seems almost entertaining to anyone,
But the sweet note of a twittering bird
Coming from afar with intense, pleasing sensation,
May have certain divine connotation - a sympathetic tone
For those poor, decrepit and suffering
Outdoors, having no resources at all!
Yet, the very musical tone at the moment,
Seems much elevating and stirring
To anything in that cold, drooping condition of night!

Kalyan Ray

LIFE TO DEATH; THAT SHORT SPACE

Life, hanging together with discarded
string and sticky tape. On the edge,
string worn ragged and tape crinkled.
But if the right word is spoken, the
word that washes clean, then, for a
brief moment it all turns to gold.
Yet this will not last. It will
soon end. With rope and chair!

Godfrey Dodds

A GYPSY'S THUMB

My mum was special
She was a gardener
She could make anything grow
You know?

My mum was exceptional
She could plant anything in the soil
Magically turning it into loveliness
Bursting into fruitfulness and life

My mum was carefree
She would leave the dishes in the sink
And go outside into the garden
No matter the hour or the day

My mum was remarkable
She could turn her memories into seeds
Planting them gently in my mind
To nurture, grow, forever to be plucked

My mum was amazing
A bright mosaic, full of fun
A collage of her past, my future
And grows on in my daughter and my son

My mum was special
She was a gardener
With a gypsy's thumb
My mum.

Sue Percival

RAINBOW IN THE SKY

Somewhere there is a rainbow in the sky,
And I will find my true love there.
Until that day I shall plod along,
And make my way to where?

Why then is it, as it is,
I question every day.
That then is how it has to be,
As everyone knows the way.

A life which is unique,
Means everything to me.
This is the way of the world,
And how it has to be.

How can we aim to please,
If the questions are not right?
Are we here today, to ask this,
And question our own plight?

I plod along and know that's why,
I do what I must do.
For I see a rainbow up ahead,
And underneath is you.

Dawn Graham

REALITY

I dream of you
With my eyes wide open
To hear your voice
And feel your touch
Fill me with ecstasy
But you're not there
Memories are all I have
Of a love once warm
But now grown cold.

Alice Higham

VALENTINE LOVE

When our eyes meet,
When we touch,
The love is a-tender, for heart to render.
When we kiss on a rainy day
It makes me shine with rays of light.
I would love you on a cold night.
Take all your pain away,
For love is love and love I must,
Is it right, is it wrong?
For I know that we belong.
You walk so gently, you talk so sweet,
The sun that shines on dark thoughts
Melts the cold and only in love are we taught.
When I feel like this, an angel from above
Soars to hold you, hold me too,
For times like this are few.
You smell fresh like a red rose
I want you to be unfrozen and then
You will be my special sweet Valentine,
To love on a sunny day,
For hearts to ignite in a magical way.

Paul Billett

TIME IS FOR YOU

It's strange how
When we are older
The days and the months
Seem to fly
Your joints creak a little
You can't move so fast
And life seems to be
Passing you by
Don't hang in the doldrums
Think positive thoughts
Get out in the world
When you can
You have so much to give
Look at all you've achieved
Most everything that's known to man
Time is for you
To make what you can
It's a wonderful time to explore
You will be surprised
There is so much to do
You just have to go through your door.

Jeanette Gaffney

PICKED UP AND RUN WITH

Matthew Arnold school inspector
left Philistia a defector
broke with philhellenic custom
made a hero out of Rustum
modelled him on dear old daddy –
scholar, filicide and baddy?

David Fitzsydney

IN MY LIFE
(Dedicated to Sue Nicholson)

The stars at night
shone so bright
when you were in my life,
the sun glistened in your eyes
I thought I was in paradise,
All I wanted was for you to be my wife.

In my life I've dreamt of
having that someone special,
I thought you were the one
But it just wasn't meant to be,
I showered you with gifts
and wrote you love poems,
but it just wasn't enough.

I dream of you every night,
from when the stars come out
until the sun shines bright,
everything was fine,
I thought you'd always be mine,
but then you just turned your back on me
and now I have no one in my life.

Chris T Barber

GRAVESEND

Why Gravesend?
Is it such a dismal place
That they should name it so?

I've never been there -
But it makes me think
That I should go and see
If this is how it's meant to be -
I'm off to buy a ticket!

Welcome to Kent, 'Garden Of England',
Beauty abounds everywhere.
You may never want to leave!

M Fitzpatrick-Jones

STANDING IN THE SHADOWS

Have you been listening to me
In the last hour?
Thought I heard you say
That I had no power.
Have you been thinking of me
In the last hour,
Trying to forget that
I have some power.
See me there,
Standing in the shadows,
It makes me feel lost, at a cost,
So I may as well
Break on through.

Wendy Day

YOUR ACHIEVEMENT

Now you have them
where you want them -
analogue-brained with
digital spending power -

All decorated wrinkles;
like Christmas trees
on New Year's Eve.

You will remember how
mono was always
sharper and more incisive
than stereo -

and you will be
quietly satisfied
at your achievement.

Peter Asher

THE HIRING

All I need now is a darling wife.
To find one is hard you know.
To court one and wed one I do not have the time.
What woman wants to work from dawn to dusk? Cooking and slaving.
So, to the hiring market I must go.
A fine lass I may pick up, you never know.
Plump or skinny, it matters not, so long as
I win her favours and she obeys my every whim.
Hope she is a good cook. You know all she has to do.
Milk the cows, feed the pigs and hens,
Bake the bread, clean the wee house, press my Sunday best.
Must look good in the pub.
God, would murder for a pint of the black stuff.
Here they come. Fancy the wee red-haired one.
Five bob a week and her keep.
Hm. That chubby one, not bad. 7/6 a week. No way.
Now the blonde. Looks good. Good bearing hips.
Might get a few sons there. Maybe a girl or two.
Could flog them off myself. Now there's a thought.
Ten bob a week. No matter, beggars cannot be choosers.
Hope I get a year out of her.
Last one. Only got a week out of her. I wonder why?

Norman Andrew Downie

ENIGMA

I find myself in a dilemma
And cannot understand my feeling
She is an enigma
Should I quell this urge
And quash the surge of emotion
She is an enigma

Should I purge the notion that she cares
She is an enigma
Her ruby lips and shapely hips
She is an enigma.

S Friede

ALL THE WRONG PIECES

Anarchy in bus queues;
Assault-by-default
on rush hour trains

Death on the roads;
Date rape in bars;
Gun law on the streets

Perverts coasting;
Hypocrites anxiously taking
Communion

Disabled access leaving
much to be desired;
Gays, blasted

People in self-imposed
segregation, making the most
of whatever legislation

Society's jigsaw parts
little more than thoughtlessly
discarded litter.

R N Taber

IF YOU LOOK AT THE SKY AT NIGHT YOU'LL BE SURPRISED!

Too many lights! Light from the stars, light from the moon!
They all beam down to us at night.
The sky is full of many things: stars and galaxies and planets.
Who knows what else is there? Nobody knows.
But I think that up there is someone who knows everything,
But he will not tell us because it is a big, complicated mystery.
The sky is so big it is an immensity of space and mystery,
But it is so lovely to look at night.
The moon and his brilliant lights,
All the sky is an intrigue for my eye.
It would be nicer if I could understand,
But since I am ignorant of the fact,
I'll never be clever enough to discover the mystery of the sky.
I still say that someone knows, because I am sure
That all things that are in the sky he put there
And he knows too well and he still controls them.
For all of us it is a mystery, but for him all is clear.
The scientist goes crazy thinking, but for him it is so simple.
I say this, forget the scientist and trust him.
He is the supreme divine and with him,
Everything will be right and clear.

Antonio Martorelli

SNOW

The soft white flakes fall slow . . .
the perfect Christmas scene in March
to show.

Thick flakes fall more rapid and dense.
Silence holds one in suspense; begging
young and old observe the falling feathery puffs.

It's uncommon to us, this snow.
The little ones instinctively know
what to do to explore its many realms.

Every child's spirit soars.
To make that snowball, snowman,
snow sledge . . . slithering, sliding, glow
and glare, a cloud of breath in the cold
bright air.

The cold sets in. The run to the blazing
heat to warm up aching fingertips and feet.
The children revel in the fun.
In and out of the house in wet and soggy clothes.

A blanket of white when trampled turns to
slush; a horrid unsightly mess.
But, for now a soft covering veil on treetops,
roofs and garden fence. The night will bring
the ice.

The bitter cold disappears with descending
accumulating maze. The silent hush plugs the
ears, drawing the senses to a point, sky of
hazy, misty pale.

This can't be happening so near the sea.

Marie McCarthy

THE JACKAL

The jackal will loathe none,
As loathe the unseen eagle,
For seeing him.

Tom Hathaway

A WEEKEND TOGETHER

Weekends, time to relax and unwind. Theatre, cinema, reading, writing, shopping, browsing in bookshops, relaxing in coffee shops, restaurants, a walk in the park and so much more.

But one thing is missing for you are not there, the only person I would like to share my weekends with.

We are apart at weekends, you and I, such a shame for two people with so many similar interests.

Then, on Mondays, we tell each other all about our separate pursuits, what we have been doing.

Oh, how I wish we could be together for a weekend, enjoying one another's company, laughing and joking. No need, then, to relate what we got up to after the event.

My sweet darling, please say you will spend a weekend with me soon because I am sure it would bring us closer together.

Life is too short for us to be apart much longer . . .

Nash

BABY, BABY

Oh baby, baby, don't stand there,
Come along, get on board, get a life
Catch the train, we're all on board, don't miss this chance.
Don't miss the train, you'll sure regret it if you do.
What the hell are you gonna do?

Oh baby, baby, please don't stand there.
Don't leave me weeping, please leap on in.
The train is leaving, the horns are blowing.
We're all going for a ride somewhere in the sun.
Leave all the fools behind, step right on up.
This is special, this is real, this train takes you to another level.
The driver tells me, it's a pick you up,
A tonic to some other dimension.
They strap you in, because this train flies, yeah, really flies,
Right up to another sky.

Oh baby, baby, just don't stand there,
Let's shoot on up to a great new life.
Will you please be my wife? What's that you say?
Yes, you will! Oh baby, what a thrill.
That's right girl, step on up, take my hand,
I've got the tickets for our great new life.

Terry Ramanouski

LOVE, THROUGH LIFE AND DEATH

Within this life,
All the love remembered.
More, than the wealth it brings.
Now with life, surrendered,
Share all your love
With the King of kings.

John Robinson

JANUARY SNOW

Here it comes, look beside
The lamp, it's bleaching down.
We are in for a bad few days.
Here come the grit lorries.
God bless their cotton socks.
The drivers are going slow.
Here comes the cold, biting
My fingers and toes.

I'll be taking a hot water bottle
To bed tonight, to cuddle,
And feel like toast.
Here are the ice and car tracks,
Here is the wet umbrella in the bath,
Here are the footprints to my door,
Here is the snowman in the street.

Kenneth Mood

THE MACROCARPA TREES

Learning *more* of trees! An expert 'name',
The skies, an indicated - form;
'Point-to-these, should my clouds want fame,'
And, 'Dare you point the cries-of-storm?'

And, if you come to understand
The eventful climb I enter on,
It is like shaking nature's hand
To feel your rich adherents cooled,
And so, so-schooled, with-loving-done!

For:
As a boy, I'd use my shins
And scale the bunches near the stems
And, wear my hair in diadems:
The apex of your point, 'who wins.'

But never would this gentle tip
Be reached, for, always from the top,
The knitted lace of twigs my crown
Would push awry, and I should stop.

And, if a lonely lad may say,
'I climbed my "olde macarp" today,'
He'll follow, where he comes entribed,
The rich, dark green to you ascribed.

(Boy speaks),
'*And* feel the resin with my thumb,
Sticky on the cheese-rind bark;
And from my grip, the fingers numb:
For me our sleep is soap to come;
Goodbye, and Heaven is a spark.'

R D Westlake-Clayton-Sackett

AUTISM!

I look into your eyes
Where are you now?
Are you with us, John Joe,
Or in a world of your own?
What do you think about?
Are you happy,
Are you free,
Do you know what hurt is?
Do you like my touch,
My hugs,
My kisses?
Do you know you're my son,
Do you know I am your mother?
In my eyes you are everything.
Let me into your mind
For one minute.
I want to feel what you feel,
I want to know what it is like
Being you!

Geraldine McMullan Doherty

YOUR LETTER

In my briefcase your letter
hidden in the pages of a Sunday supplement
which I will read again and again
and feel your hand on my face,
smell your perfume in a room you have just left.
And I will hold my breath,
see you sitting there
your feet not touching the ground
and I will close my eyes, then, remember,
how you grew up
and we grew apart.
Now a lie
is my ride to the airport,
where your plane will touch down
on the raw flesh of my past.

Peter Herridge

ON THIS DAY, THE FIRST OF MAY

We are throwing a party,
A special guest is coming.
The celebration to be seen
All over the teeming world.
There's 24 hour TV coverage
With our guest's arrival,
A day of frivolity and feasting
And numerous religious services,
Prayers said in churches
Linked around the globe.
We want everything to be perfect.
It seems the whole Earth
Is thrilled by this unique visit.
I've never seen so many happy faces.
There's speeches to be made
By our leaders in the United nations.
The stable set looks immaculate,
Including the farmyard beasts.
They too, seem aware of the occasion,
From cattle, sheep and goats,
To the humble domestic chickens.
They're all on their best behaviour,
On this very special day in May.
Many folk have reported seeing angels.
You're right, everyone now has heard
Of course, it's the living Lord Jesus,
On the occasion of His second coming,
From the celestial stairs descending.
Trumpets - Heaven's gate thrown wide open,
Here comes the Prince of Peace and Love.

Jonathan Pegg

9/11

It has been three years
Since that awful day,
Now we stand
And now we pray
For *oh* so many lives,
Needlessly taken away.
It has been three long years
Since
That tragic day.

Megan Beth

PIN-UPS

A pin for this,
a pin for that,
a pin for the other,
What's the number? Oh drat!

Can't think? Don't fret
Down at the pub
We've a super idea
For a new *pin-up* club!

Not *that* sort dear,
But an 'oldies' one.
We'll write to dear Tony
Let him know it's no fun.

What's the number for this,
What's the number for that,
What's the one for the other?
We forget, that's a fact.

Wait till *you're* old, Tony,
And *your* mind's gone astray -
You'll bemoan what you've done
To we oldies today.

What's *your* number for this,
What's *your* number for that,
What's the one for *your* other?
You won't get it off pat.

You'll be too old
Like the rest of us,
You'll only be able
To sit down and cuss!

And serve you right too!

Paddy Jupp

MY HOME

My home is full of love,
For all my family to share.

My home is full of happiness,
Christmas time is one of the best.

My home is full of glee,
It's full of high spirits and liveliness.

My home is full of warmth,
Through all the four seasons.

My home is full of tenderness,
Compassion and sympathy when things go bad.

My home is full of joy,
Every day is like a summer's day.

My home is full of contentment,
There's no place like home.

My home is full of sadness.
When I grew up and moved.

Catrina Lawrence

OPEN AND DIRECT

Sweeping past each field o'er fen
Draining marsh
And home of heron -
River lined by feathered rush
Running swift
And flowing fast
In channels cut
With banks built high
Flows like gold
'Neath endless sky.
Waterway
Drain and dyke
By land so rich
And above
Skylark
Lapwing, curlew
Moorhen, coot
The mallard duck -
They glide
They speak
To all who here
Live by spirit
From far and near.
The freedom which this land so calls
As the cry of nature
In her wisdom
Rules.

Lyn Sandford

FOG

The sun that warmed the sea and land throughout the day has gone,
And now the swirling, rolling fog invades the shore.
The waves still break upon the sand, but now unseen, just heard,
Whilst swooping seabirds' piercing cries are heard no more.

Great ships, far out to sea, have slowed, and doubled crew on watch,
Who strain their ears for sounds of foghorn's echoing boom,
As though their eyes before have seen a far off storm's approach,
Not one can see beyond this choking cloud of doom.

Ashore the creeping mist grows denser, suffocating lungs,
pervading every building, seeping through the cracks,
While street lamps' weakened rays mutate within this 'smoke',
And dripping condensation marks its tracks.

A shaft of light spills from the tavern door, across the path
To an old newspaper, in the gutter, sodden,
Its news forgot, its pictures too, the pages can't be read,
The only 'print' to see, is where a foot has trodden.

Dawn breaks, the new sun rises, warming breezes from the land,
Night's phantom shapes become revealed - bush, hedge - a tree.
No longer mute, grey seals', and seabirds' songs are heard again,
And mariners' great ships are safe, once more, at sea.

Geoffrey Leech

TO CHIARA

What is a face?
What is a face
Against the trace of time?
What are a pair
Of lips against
The rose?
What is a smile
Against a
Sunrise?
What is a face
Against the
Trace of time?
The answer is
Nothing,
Unless that
Face is thine.

David A Bray

WONDERING

The slow dripped away wisdom of the years
Leaving a laughable insanity
Was it all worth it?
Learning to live with disasters
Coping bravely - for what?
To save oneself for painful old age?

I had stopped off the track a few times
Cheating the conventional
That was fulfilling, the rest a real drag
Now drained of all effort
Even the sinful is too de-energising.

I am the spanner which gets in the works
Temptation to wreck the boat a constant companion
Am I part human, part mythical beast
Or just raging away at old age?
You tell me.

Joan R Gilmour

HURT

All that hurts
Is from deep inside
born at an insult
Never to die
But why people hurt
It is easy to see
A thorn in the hedge
A pin in the knee
But hurt is not a pain
That lives outside
It comes from betrayal
Like a little white lie
If we all told the truth
And benefited others
Wouldn't life be easier?
Away from denial.

Stephen Crossman

NEW DAY

A prayer,
start with a prayer.
One of thanks,
of praise.
For the good in mankind,
the care he or she
shows to others.
For the dawning
of a new day.
For the love
revealing itself, slowly,
throughout the planet
we inhabit.
A prayer of hope,
of things to come,
as yet unseen.
For the wisdom
of our elders.
The untapped life ahead.
The energy we gain,
The food we consume.

We thank you
for allowing us
to live another day.
Another new day.
The start
of time
to be spent
with care.

C Webb

ILL

Eve stood
                    in
        positions
            of
                        severe
sadness
                    keep
            heavy
        why
        face
sorrow
unspeakable?

Alex Warner

PIGEON POEM

The pigeon situation
Is a starving exclamation.
I have no reservations
When I say,
'Don't feed the pigeons.'

For they have a reputation
With aggressive inclinations.
If they don't get,
Regular food concessions.

But you can't help feeling pity for them
Pecking at the ground
For tiny scraps of nothing
Because a lack of food they've found.

It's hard surviving nature's inclement seasons
And human death trap devices.
There is a wave of great fatalities
In the pigeon population,
With cats and dogs upon them.

Trapped in a world of pollution
Where they have no words to complain.
Cruel people try to catch them
Making money out of horrible pigeon pie.
A pigeon's life can be hard
That, no one can deny!

Ali Sebastian

A CONVERSATION AT THE BUS STOP

She crossed from Netto, she seemed rather old
Funeral flowers were laid neatly nearby my house.
We started chatting. 'Hello love, by god it's cold,
Some poor soul's final journey, without a doubt.
That's where we all end up, there's nought to be done,
It's nothing to do with booze or fags, it's down to fate.'
'Do you really think so?'
'Oh yes, pet, death's no fun.'
'Well how come women hang on for years, they seem to die late?'
'Women are made differently dear, we hang on
Because we're stronger than men, got things to do.
My old man was as fit as a fiddle then suddenly, gone.
Perhaps longevity is only meant for the elite few?'
'I've never looked at it like that, but we all die, it's inevitable.'
'You're right, but when you think about it,
Being alive is quite incredible.'

Ann Hathaway

MIST

Mist,
Encircling,
Robs the morning of its true glory.
Cloud,
Descending,
Engulfs all in its waterfall haze.
Then,
Suddenly,
Returns to the ether whence it came.

Alex L Jones

THE HOME PLATE

A scourge this place
People will die here
Never being reborn
Except in the mind
Concepts will burn out
To be replaced by brains
Inertly speculating
On their next cigarette
And cup of coffee
Conversation will die out
To be replaced by mindless music
And there will be no happiness
Eternal salvation
Will crucify those of us
Still on the cross
So come down and rage against them
They are dead
Laughing in the other room
Calculating monsters
Oh the feelings you say
What are they
What kind of man is this
I say I hurt
I say I turn hot and cold
And that I am neurotic
Wouldn't you be
But then again why be so sorry
If no one responds
After all this is only a poem
Then those who say that
Don't know a poem
From a hand grenade

Under their heads
And it goes off
That heart we are all supposed to have
Spills over the floor.

Dave St Clair

TWO BIRDS IN SONG

A blue tit sang up on a bough
Rejoicing merrily, loud and sweet.
A raven perched close to him,
Grumbling at the heat.
'No worms will come,'
He loudly croaked,
'However deep men plough.'
'Glorious is the sunshine'
Sang the blue tit on the bough.
'Oh! Do be quiet,' the raven croaked
And shook his feathers crossly.
Thunder clouds were threatening,
The skies were overcast
And heavy rain was falling,
Hard and fast.
'Where's your sunshine now?'
Croaked the raven.
'Behind the clouds,' the blue tit
Happily sang up on the bough.
'Well! I'll fly behind the clouds to see
And prove you wrong, I vow!'
He spread his wings to go.
'No! You won't!
You'll find the sun is always shining,'
Sang the blue tit on the bough.

Doreen Petherick Cox

UNTITLED

Who do you
have to be
to stay out
of trouble?
A 'copper' or
an MP,
a soldier or
some rubble?
How long
will it be
before I get
into trouble?
At 17 or 45?
While
next door's
drinking doubles.

Philip Allen

WISPS AND STORM CLOUDS

The smallest of clouds is sometimes the timid, old woman,
Like the impolite,
She is always expected but never shows,
Though often she summons the courage
To brave the heat of the sun,
Frail and wispy, old and grey, she never lingers,
Allowing the gentle breeze to quietly bear her away.

Her successor lays her down upon his fluffed-up pillow,
The patterned impressionist, he of many guises,
Stranger they became with no boundaries of sense,
The amateur philosopher's delight,
Often he prefers the sheepish kind, for he is like them,
Dozens of white flecks against the dominantly coloured background.

Sometimes she prefers a certain time of day,
On the horizon,
She meets with the sun as he slowly makes his way
Across the sky,
Completing nature's artwork,
She paints the sky many-coloured in the dawn light with her radiance.

When, at height of summer, the sun controls the sky,
He and she, the clouds,
Impatient they become, and gather all their sombre-looking armies
United in frustration,
Swiftly march the invaders on to the sun, casting him to exile,
Blockading the earth from his eye they patrol the skies,
Waiting to strike.

Full of black and threatening anger,
Voices echo
As they vent upon the suntanned ground their grievances,
Furious tears quench the land's thirst as jagged anvils strike in malice
And as the gloom's grip tightens,
So the world is changing.

Edward John David Green (15)

TOKEN REMINDERS

You did not hit me to cause my pain.
No bruises can be seen upon my body.
But yet the torture that did ensue
Caused me more pain than you will ever know.
Token reminders still haunt my life.
Silent phone calls in the dark of night.
Hateful mail full of spite.
People raised voices, caused me to run and hide.
Abuse of my mind and my self esteem.
Confidence torn from my very being.
How can I ever make a new start?
Trust does not come easy.
How I wish that it would.
Mental anguish never leaves my side.
How did I let this happen to me?
Years of believing things would change,
Always thinking I was the one to blame.
You may no longer have me under your control,
But the abuse you dealt has taken its toll.
Doctors, pills, I will try them all
If my mind will once again be free.
Therapy will rid me of your abusive hold.
One day I will no longer think of the token reminders.

Jo Lodge

THE POMEGRANATE TREE

Today I watched the death
of the pomegranate tree
it bloomed in red, all ready to fruit
instead, the chopper to cut its breath
thrust ahead
in its brute pursuit
the tree protested and refused
to come down; did its best
its only offence, the old lady
had planted it where
the new occupant's vision
of villa's elevation
was hindered
the tree obscured
the material grandeur
nature's beauty
was sacrificed
at the altar of prosperity.

Nayyer Ali

To My Dog

I can always love you freely,
you'll never reject my affections
nor question my motives
nor fall out or argue.
Pure as your smooth white coat
I know your love is unconditional.

I love your doggy smell and doleful eyes
you wag your tail, lick my nose,
talk to me with those eyes.
I might be barking mad at times
and even sad
but your love is always unconditional.

I know I mollycoddle you
and keep you on a tight leash
when you yearn to be free to roam
like your ancestors primordial.
I turn to you for comfort
because your love is unconditional.

I know you get confused
when we both vie for your affection
when our love has turned to hate.
You get perplexed when we behave so beastly,
why can't our love be unconditional?

Coral Raven

WORDS

You always know the truth
Because when you cut yourself, or someone else with it,
You bleed
The most important things
Are the hardest things to say
They are the things you get ashamed of
Because words diminish them
Words shrink the things that seem limitless in your head
But it's more important than that
The most important things lie too close
To wherever your soul is buried
And you may make revelations that cost you dearly
Only to have people not understand what you've said at all
Or why you thought it was so important
That you almost cried while saying it
That's the worst
When secrets stay locked within
For want of an understanding ear.

Sandra Simmons

GREY TO THE POWER OF ONE

Oh! The shades of grey I can describe
From the hut I sit and gaze
That long grey road that runs to Nass
Or the passing clouds, second phase
Tapping Morse with pencil's base
I tick the calendar to the holidays

I sit and wait the cold grey dawn
The milkman prompts an open gate
First comes a trickle then a throng
Unwavering, I wave, I sit, I wait
Then a lull, then comes Jonnie last
With tacit greetings we both postulate

Then a brighter grey fills the room
Importance comes by telephone
Message is, it could, it might, it may
I concur instead of moan
And so another productive day
I notice a weed in a rone

Suddenly there's a strange request
At the door, a tramp, hat doffed
Lost grey eyes and bloodstained vest
A cigarette he begs, I did not scoff
For in uniform with lanyard well pressed
In soft grey tones I tell him to f**k off.

E C Mulvaney

NOT SO RUDE AWAKENING

A creaking noise outside the door
Woke me from my deep warm sleep
Was it just a dream?
I listened hard and waited quiet,
Silly me! I thought as I closed my eyes once more,
A scratching sound with horrible noise,
Now my eyes wide with terror!
Feeling cold and not so bold,
Imagination is on fire,
Ghosts and ghouls, witches and vampires,
All of these race through my mind.
I wish it was morning coming fast,
But there's a lot of dark till half-past seven.
I pray to God who art in Heaven
Keep me safe and help me sleep.
I hide under the blankets,
Then the hellish sound moves closer.
I start to sweat with heartbeat's pace,
I feel a hand touching me,
I start to scream as the blankets are flung from me.
To my relief it is my mother I discover,
'Morning dear, had a bad dream?'

Daren Armstrong

WHO ARE THEY KIDDING?

Dancing round the magic roundabout
Dougal got poor Florence up the spout.
A large hump was clear to see
What a shock for poor Zebedee.
There was this lump there on show,
A prize at the end of the rainbow.
The weather too was getting so whippy,
They all decided to hide in Zippy.

How can she face life without a spouse?
Could she find a room in Hector's House?
Florence told the press a sad story,
How it all took place on pretty Balamory.
If Dougal found out he would kill her.
Did she not have a week with Bob The Builder?
They say we must not blame a cat,
I still feel it was down to a Rugrat.

Colin Allsop

THE BELL

It didn't seem important,
This ceramic doll bell,
When you bought it
For a couple of pence

Every Tuesday,
You took it to your centre,
And didn't care less,
What anyone thought,
You would take it out,
And ring it again and again,
Hinting that it was time for tea
Everyone would giggle
And everyone would laugh,
And the sadness would lift
From their eyes for a moment

It didn't seem important,
This ceramic doll bell,
But when you bought it
For a couple of pence,
Now that you're gone,
It seems so important to me.

A Bhambra

HANDS

Her hands lie in her lap,
each soft fold glistening
with the translucency of age.
These fingers have touched,
caressed, five babies' cheeks;
twelve more as generation
gave rise to generation.
Her palms are lined
with telling trails;
palms that have held
four lovers close,
one closer still.
A band of gold sits, loose now,
where he placed it
over sixty years ago,
the memory fresh,
as is that of his last smile.
The quiet of the room
surrounds her and calms the air
and the hands lie still,
browned by many summers,
her memories not dulled
by the passing of
so many winters.
Her smile will linger
long after her passing.
Other hands will wear her ring,
hold the photographs,
caress her treasures,
breathe life into the memory of her.

Karen Barron

POISON IVY

Ivy, congruous with racial tolerance
tightens grip on world bigotry.
Elongated tentacles creep forward
in a sure choking journey.

Parasitic tongues grow long
to poison minds of unwary listener.
Prejudice, entrenched in cancerous roots
eventually succumb and depress,
poison ivy has finished its journey.

Alex Branthwaite

I'LL FOREVER LOVE THE ONES CLOSE TO MY HEART BUT FOREVER HATE EVERYTHING ABOUT ME

Tired and alone we feel so cold
Memories frozen, our misfortune told
Stones in our hearts leave broken bones
Happiness lost in all we shared

Time's way of changing day by day
Mood swings devalue face, sometimes our race
Are we able now to give a chase
To what people may seem as a worthless case?

My glands stumble, delaying, nowhere to stay
Our bodies ache in these helpless times of changing
I cannot lay beside you, you've been taken away
We are left parted, far apart now tears have started

Looking back in twenty years what will you feel?
Will you cry when you begin to look upon me?
I'm tying down my hands around this tree
Loving always made me sparkle with glee

Now this frost has bitten my life, now it stings
Unable to warm in what the summer brings
Love in air is my eternally winter in the air
Now I've lost you, will summer be the evil stare?

Jason Bone

A Drinker's Tale

A drink is all that's on my mind
a liquid strong and fast,
something that can drown my thoughts
forget what's in the past,
I know I'm drinking quite a lot
it's hard to self confess,
I'm looking in a mirror
and someone's looking back at me,
to see the details on that face
I know it's me I'm looking at
but yet it's someone else,
I hate myself, I want to die
but still I seem to live my life,
looking down the neck
into an empty bottle
that makes me what I am
and what I can't confess.

Joseph Jezierski

SUBMISSIONS INVITED
SOMETHING FOR EVERYONE

OVER £10,000 POETRY PRIZES
TO BE WON!

POETRY NOW 2004 - Any subject,
any style, any time.

WOMENSWORDS 2004 - Strictly women,
have your say the female way!

STRONGWORDS 2004 - Warning!
Opinionated and have strong views.
(Not for the faint-hearted)

All poems no longer than 30 lines.
Always welcome! No fee!
Cash Prizes to be won!

Mark your envelope (eg *Poetry Now*) *2004*
Send to:
Forward Press Ltd
Remus House, Coltsfoot Drive,
Peterborough, PE2 9JX
(01733) 898101

If you would like to order further copies of this
book or any of our other titles, please give us a
call or log onto our website at
www.forwardpress.co.uk